GO FACT

Sea Life

Blake
EDUCATION
ways to learn

Sea Life

contents

Go Facts
Sea Life
ISBN: 1-86509-469-2

Copyright © 2002 Blake Publishing
Published by Blake Education Pty Ltd
ABN 074 266 023
Locked Bag 2022
Glebe NSW 2037

Ph (02) 8585 4085
Fax (02) 8585 4058

Email: mail@blake.com.au
Website: askblake.com.au

Written by Katy Pike, Garda Turner
Science Consultant: Dr. Will Edwards, James Cook University
Design and layout by The Modern Art Production Group
Photos by Photodisc, Stockbyte, John Foxx, Corbis, Imagin, Artville,
Digital Vision and Corel
Printed By Green Giant Press

Fish

Fish are animals that live in water and can swim. All fish have a backbone, gills and fins.

The oceans cover more than two-thirds of the earth. Where there is life in the ocean, you will find fish. Fish live, swim, breathe and breed under water.

The bodies of fish are made for life under water. Smooth bodies, fins and strong tails make swimming easy. The gills on a fish work like our lungs. The fish takes in water through its mouth and the gills **absorb** the oxygen from the water.

Bony Fish

The most common fish are bony fish. Bony fish have skeletons and jaws made of bone. Scales cover their bodies. Tuna, salmon and goldfish are all bony fish with fanlike fins.

Bony fish can stop swimming and not sink to the bottom. Inside each fish is a swim bladder that contains air, like a balloon. The fish can inflate the swim bladder to float higher in the water or deflate it to swim into deeper water.

Fish can swim in large schools.

Snappers are carnivores.

Barracudas have strong, bony jaws for catching food.

Sharks

Sharks are fish with skeletons made of cartilage, not bone. Instead of scales, sharks have skin that is rough and scratchy.

Sharks have long, **streamlined** bodies with thick, stiff fins. These fins are very different from the spiny, fanlike fins of other fish.

Sharks swim by moving their strong tails from side to side. Because they do not have a swim bladder, sharks must keep swimming or they will sink.

Some sharks, such as the great white shark, are fierce predators. Using all of their senses, they hunt and eat fish, squid and other sea creatures. Sharks' powerful jaws and sharp, triangular teeth take large bites out of their prey.

Other sharks are **filter** feeders. Sea water enters their large open mouths and flows through a mesh attached to their gills. **Plankton** and other sea creatures get caught in this fine net. The world's largest fish, the whale shark, feeds this way.

Whale sharks are the largest fish.

The great white shark is a fierce predator.

Whitetip reef sharks find food on the sea floor.

GO FACTS

LARGEST FISH!

The whale shark can be as long as five cars.

7

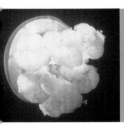

Creatures That Sting

Some sea creatures have stinging tentacles. They use these to kill their prey. Jellyfish, sea anemones and coral polyps are animals with tentacles. These animals have no bones.

Jellyfish have very soft bodies that are almost **transparent**. They have no bones, eyes, hearts or brains but they can sense which way is up. Swimming upwards, jellyfish follow plankton, their main source of food. Jellyfish have long **tentacles** that they use like fishing lines to catch food.

Sea anemones also have tentacles. The tentacles look like flower petals but they contain poison. An anemone pulls food into its mouth using its tentacles.

Millions of tiny animals called coral **polyps** form coral reefs. The stinging tentacles that surround the polyps' mouths can stretch out to catch food. Coral polyps make a hard outer casing to protect themselves. This rocklike casing remains after the animals die, building up coral reefs.

sea anemone

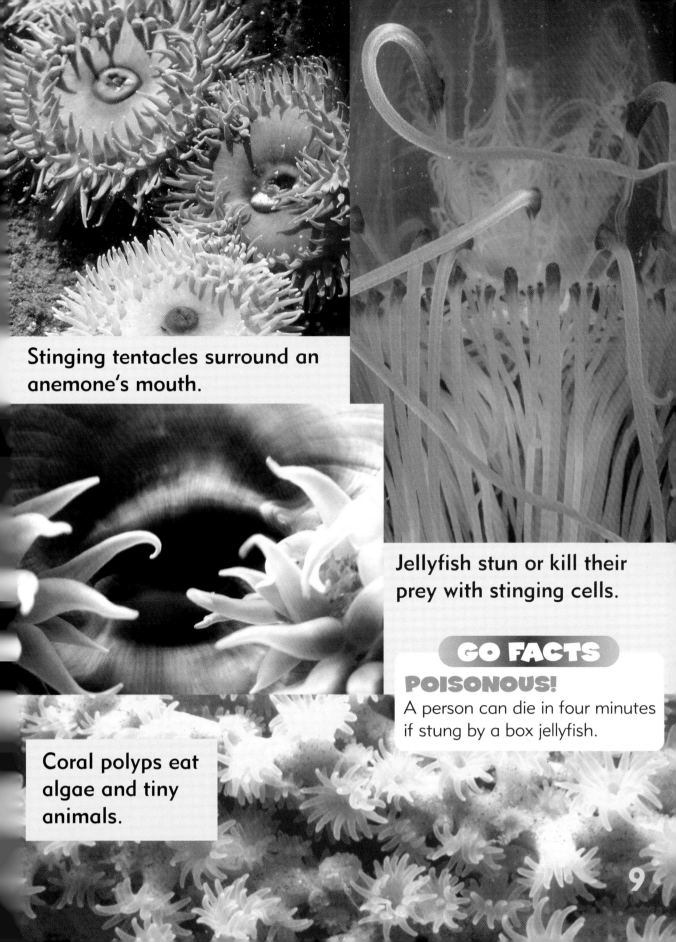

Stinging tentacles surround an anemone's mouth.

Jellyfish stun or kill their prey with stinging cells.

GO FACTS

POISONOUS!
A person can die in four minutes if stung by a box jellyfish.

Coral polyps eat algae and tiny animals.

9

Starfish

Starfish are predators. Most of them live in shallow water. Starfish have five or more arms and are covered with a rough, hard skin.

Starfish have arms that spread out in the shape of a star. Many starfish have five arms but they can have up to 18 arms. If an arm breaks off, it can regrow.

Each arm has rows of **tube feet** that can fasten onto rocks like suction cups. When they grip a rock firmly, even big waves will not move them.

Starfish are very successful predators. They eat many sea creatures, such as worms, clams, coral and crabs.

The mouth of a starfish is on the underside of its body, in the centre. The starfish wraps itself around a clam and uses its tube feet to pull the shell open. Then the starfish pushes its stomach out through its mouth and into the shell to eat the clam.

The tube feet of starfish are very strong.

Starfish move slowly.

Starfish sometimes eat fish out of fishing nets.

11

Crustaceans

Crustaceans have their skeletons on the outside. These hard shells cover and protect their bodies. Crabs, prawns and barnacles are all crustaceans.

Crabs have hard, flat shells and five pairs of legs. The two front legs have claws that can pick up and carry things. The other legs bend sideways under the crab's body. This is why crabs walk and run sideways.

Shrimps, prawns and krill are like the insects of the sea, small and numerous. Shells cover their jointed bodies and ten pairs of legs. They can beat their tails to swim quickly through the water.

Krill look like tiny shrimps. Large swarms of krill live in cool oceans. Each swarm can be made up of millions of animals. The world's largest animal, the blue whale, feeds mainly on krill.

Barnacles attach themselves to rocks or other hard surfaces. When they open their shells, feathery arms reach out to attract and catch food.

Crabs can use their claws as weapons when they fight.

Hermit crabs live in empty sea snail shells.

Shrimps are one of the most common types of crustacean.

GO FACTS

LARGEST!

The giant spider crab can measure 3·7 metres between its outstretched legs.

Squids and Octopuses

Squids and octopuses are soft-bodied sea creatures called molluscs. They have tentacles for catching their prey.

Squids and octopuses have large eyes and long tentacles. Each tentacle has rows of grasping suckers that can hold onto rocks or catch prey. These two **molluscs** have mouths with sharp, filelike teeth. They use them to grind through the shells of crabs and other sea creatures that they catch.

Octopuses hide under rocks and in caves on the seabed. Hunting mainly at night, they use their eight long tentacles to catch and grip prey. Squids swim in large schools and use their ten tentacles to catch fish and other prey.

Squids and octopuses use speed to escape from predators. They both have a sacklike body that can be filled with water. To escape, they force the water out and jet off quickly. They can also squirt out clouds of ink to confuse an enemy.

Squids' large eyes help them to see in dark ocean depths.

Squids attach their egg sacks to the ocean floor.

This octopus is eating crabs and scallops.

GO FACTS

LARGEST!

The giant squid is the largest mollusc. It can grow to 17 metres long.

15

Marine Mammals

Whales, dolphins, seals and sea lions are marine mammals. Like all mammals, they give birth to live babies.

Mammals cannot breathe under water because they have lungs, not gills. They must come to the surface to breathe.

Whales and dolphins breathe through blowholes on the tops of their heads. They can dive deeply on a single breath. The babies of whales and dolphins are born under water. The mothers push the babies to the surface to take their first breath.

sea lion

Seals and sea lions have strong flippers and are good swimmers. They spend most of their time in the water, feeding on fish, squid and penguins. A layer of **blubber** under their skin keeps them warm. Seals and sea lions also spend time on land, resting. Seal pups are born on land and like all **marine** mammal babies, they are fed milk.

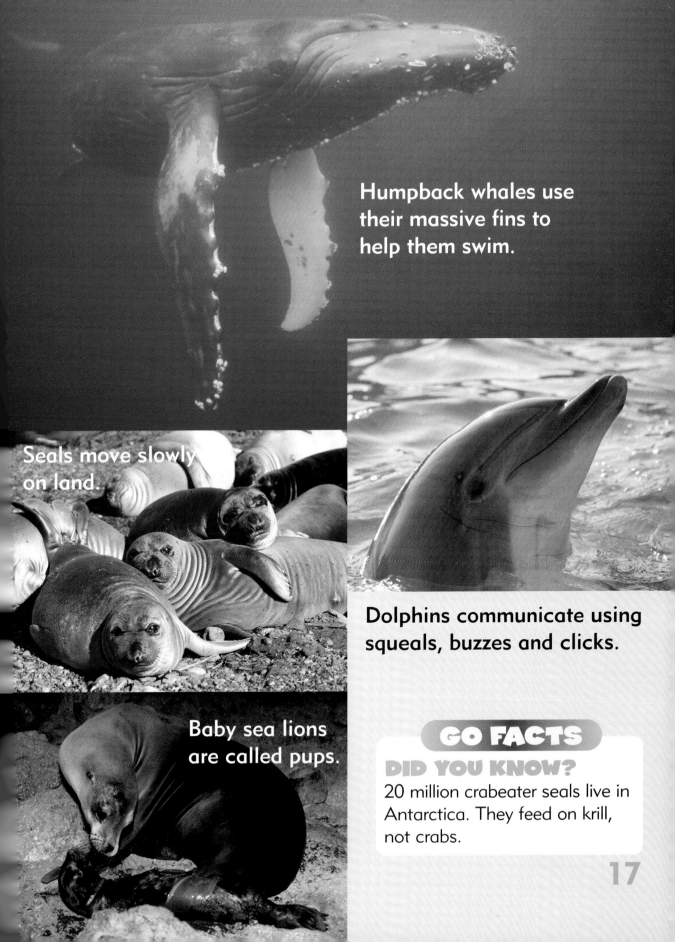

Humpback whales use their massive fins to help them swim.

Seals move slowly on land.

Dolphins communicate using squeals, buzzes and clicks.

Baby sea lions are called pups.

GO FACTS

DID YOU KNOW?

20 million crabeater seals live in Antarctica. They feed on krill, not crabs.

Seabirds

Many birds depend on the sea for their food. Wading birds, penguins, gulls and pelicans hunt and eat fish and other sea creatures.

Wading birds, such as oystercatchers, live and feed along the shore. Long, spindly legs help them to wade through shallow water. Their thin beaks dig around for small animals in the water and mud.

Out over the deeper ocean, birds need to be able to fly for long periods of time. The albatross has very long wings so that it can glide for hours. It can stay in the air for weeks at a time. These seabirds dive into the water to catch their food.

seagull

Penguins cannot fly at all. They use their flippers and their webbed feet to swim very fast and catch fish.

All seabirds nest on land. Some nest on cliffs to be safe, laying their eggs on rocks. Some build nests from sticks, others from seaweed and mud.

Pelicans use their large beaks to catch fish.

An avocet is a shorebird that feeds on tiny worms and shrimps.

Oystercatchers feed close to the shore.

Albatrosses come to land to nest.

GO FACTS

DID YOU KNOW?

Seabirds never need to drink fresh water. They can drink salt water.

Sea Plants

Sea plants are the first link in the food chains of the ocean. Seagrass and algae are the two main types of sea plants.

Seagrasses are flowering plants. They have leaves, stems, flowers and seeds. Dugongs, the cows of the sea, graze on seagrass. Turtles eat seagrass too.

Seaweed is a type of algae. As they need sunlight to grow, most seaweed grows close to the shore. To keep from being washed ashore, seaweed have holdfasts that hold onto rocks or the seabed.

Some seaweed, such as giant kelp, grows into huge underwater forests. Seals can hide from predators in kelp forests. Sea lions search through the kelp for clams, crabs and fish to eat.

Algae can also be very tiny. Some of the microscopic plankton that float in the ocean are algae. Sea animals, such as krill and other tiny crustaceans, eat algae.

Dugongs feed on seagrasses.

Lots of fish live in kelp forests.

Fish hide in plants to escape from predators.

21

Sea Life

Fish

Jellyfish and other stinging creatures

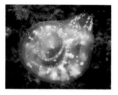    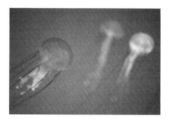

Starfish and crustaceans

 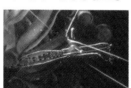   

Molluscs

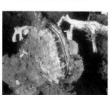    

Marine mammals

Glossary

absorb	take in
blubber	a layer of fat under the skin
cartilage	a strong and flexible substance like bone
filter	separate solids from liquids
mammal	a warm-blooded animal that gives birth to live young
marine	relating to the sea
mollusc	a sea creature with a soft body
plankton	microscopic life that floats in sea water
polyp	the sea animal that creates coral
streamlined	shaped to move quickly
tentacles	long, flexible, armlike limbs
transparent	can be seen through
tube feet	tiny feet with suction cups that starfish have

Index